Kindred Spirits
Shilombish Ittibachvffa

Leslie Stall Widener   Illustrated by Johnson Yazzie

Charlesbridge

1845, Ireland

A young Irish girl runs
between rows of potato plants.

Their leaves were
bright green yesterday.
Now they're wilted
and blotchy.

She pushes her hand
into the loose soil
and pulls the first potato
from the ground.

Not smooth and golden.
Slimy and dark.
The smell of rot.

"Dada!"
The girl drops the pratie.

Farmers can't explain why
fields of healthy-looking plants
changed overnight.

It is the beginning of the great hunger
that changed Ireland.

Irish Potato Famine

An extreme heat wave followed by drenching rains hit Ireland in the summer of 1845. The weather worried farmers, who relied on potato crops to feed their families.

The night before the second harvest in October, a fog rolled in. The next day, farmers discovered that a fungus had destroyed the crops. Many Irish people lost the only food they could afford.

The Irish Potato Famine lasted five years. More than a million Irish people died from starvation and disease. Another two million emigrated to Canada, the United States, and Britain.

1847, Choctaw Nation

Four thousand miles
across the Atlantic Ocean,
Choctaw people are still healing
from their own hardships.

A family leaves their cabin and
hurries through the cold rain.
They join others at the
Choctaw Agency building.
"Tushpa! We must not be late!"

The big room smells
of wet clothes.
Wood smoke.
Lamp oil.

Friends and families greet one another.
"Halito, chim achukma?"

They hear about a place called Ireland,
where families are torn apart,
removed from their homes,
and left to starve.

Wrapped in the warmth of family,
each Choctaw man, woman, and child listens.
They feel the pain of the Irish people.

Irish Tenants & English Landlords

Ireland seemed to be a fertile land of plenty. But most of the land was owned by English landlords, who hired Irish tenants to manage the farms. The farmers grew praties (potatoes) to feed their families. If crops were poor and farmers couldn't pay the rent, their landlords evicted them and destroyed their homes.

Looking Back at 1832

Mothers', fathers', and grandparents'
faces are streaked with tears
as they think about their own losses.

They think now of the anguish they felt
when their land was stolen
and their villages burned to the ground.
They'd touched
familiar twigs,
leaves,
rocks,
and the rough bark of beloved trees.

Removed by force
from the place of their ancestors,
they remember.

Choctaw people walked
six hundred miles
through snow and rain,
barefoot and half starved,
with only thin blankets for warmth.

The Trail of Tears
claimed thousands of lives.

The Trail of Tears

Under increasing pressure from the United States government, Choctaw chiefs signed the Treaty of Dancing Rabbit Creek in 1830. Choctaw traditional lands in Mississippi were traded for land in the West. White settlers began stealing Choctaw land.

Soon soldiers burned down villages, forcing Choctaw people to leave. They walked nearly six hundred miles, taking only what they could carry. By the time they finally reached Indian Territory, now called Oklahoma, many Choctaw people had frozen, starved, or died of disease.

1847, Choctaw Nation

Choctaw people reach into their pockets.
They give one hundred seventy dollars
to people in Ireland in honor of the injustice
suffered by both Nations.

Shilombish ittibachvffa.
Those who feel the same.
Kindred spirits.

Choctaw Relief for the Irish

Newspapers around the world published reports about the atrocities the Irish suffered during the potato famine.

When Choctaw people met at their agency building on March 23, 1847, and heard of the crisis in Ireland, they took up a collection. The $170 they gave is equivalent to $5,000 today, a huge sum for struggling people.

2017, Ireland

Seven generations into the future
and back across the ocean,
Ireland remembers.

Irish people tell the story
of the sacrificial gift
given by Choctaw people
to their Irish ancestors.

Ireland honors the Choctaw Nation
with a shining monument.
An empty bowl
created in memory of a time when
both Nations were hungry.

Kindred spirits
come together
in a shared spirit of hope,
self-sacrifice, and
perseverance.

Kindred Spirits

Irish sculptor Alex Pentek created the sculpture named *Kindred Spirits*. The empty bowl made of nine twenty-foot-tall eagle feathers represents the gift given by Choctaw people because they understood Irish people's suffering.

2020, Hopi Nation

Then the COVID-19 pandemic
infects the globe in 2020.
People everywhere are told,
"Stay home. Stay safe."

In the American Southwest,
two other Native Nations—
Navajo and Hopi—are greatly affected.
They are located in a vast desert area,
miles from family and friends.
Many people have no running water.

2020, Navajo Nation

It is a day's drive to buy
food and bottled water.
When fathers and mothers make the trip,
sickness returns with them.

Hospitals are few and
far from their homes.
Many who become sick
don't get well.

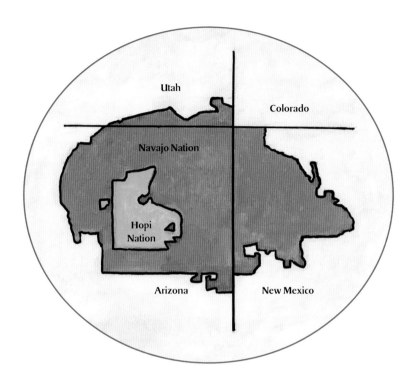

Crisis in the Southwest

COVID-19 crisscrossed the world starting in early 2020. The global pandemic devastated the sovereign Navajo and Hopi Nations, located at the Four Corners of Arizona, New Mexico, Colorado, and Utah. The United States government has repeatedly failed to provide basic and equal resources for Native people in general. During the pandemic the result was widespread suffering throughout the Navajo and Hopi Nations.

2020, Ireland

News travels quickly.
People in Ireland hear of the
suffering of the
Navajo and Hopi people.

More than twenty-six thousand Irish people
donate—many citing the Choctaw-Irish connection,
honoring their ancestors
and showing how one act of kindness can grow.
They help the Navajo and Hopi Nations.

In Ireland, a mother and daughter
gaze at the shining sculpture in the empty park.
They remember the story of how the
Choctaw Nation helped their ancestors.

From her pocket,
the girl pulls out a coin sent by her mámámó.
"Ma, I want to help."

Kindness Comes Full Circle

Members of the Navajo and Hopi Nations established a fundraising effort in March 2020 to help their people. They hoped to raise money for food and bottled water.

Over three million dollars was donated by Irish people to the Navajo and Hopi Nations. The money was given by many with ancestors who received the gift that Choctaws gave to Ireland during the potato famine.

Today and Always

Seven generations in the past,
this circle of kindness began.

Choctaw, Irish, Navajo, and Hopi.
Four Nations. Two continents.
Different, but the same.

Unified by empathy learned from hardship.
They pass generosity and compassion on
as kindred spirits.

AUTHOR'S NOTE

I'm a member of the Choctaw Nation of Oklahoma. I first heard of the Choctaw-Irish connection in summer 2017. Coworkers visited Ireland to attend the *Kindred Spirits* sculpture dedication. When they returned, I was intrigued by their stories and began researching the event that led to this honor. COVID-19 added another layer to the story, and I believe additional layers will happen in the future.

Two Nations showed empathy and compassion toward strangers and created a lasting impression on both Nations for nearly two hundred years. Good deeds from the heart, large or small, often have far-reaching effects that no one can anticipate.

ILLUSTRATOR'S NOTE

The first being was the golden eagle, Atsaa. When newcomers arrived in the Navajos' serene Southwestern world, they named it White World. Atsaa was territorial, so it created two challenges for the newcomers: waves of water and arrows. The people survived and Atsaa conceded. He relocated to the heavens and told the holy people to share and nurture White World. Atsaa's scale represents equality. The universe, nature, tradition, and the first beings bestowed law and order on the people to protect them and allow lives of harmony, peace, and balance. The *Kindred Spirit* sculpture is painted above Atsaa's head.

CHOCTAW TRAIL of TEARS and DEATH

Prior to 1830, the United States government assured Choctaw people in the Southeast that they could keep their land, provided they showed a title of ownership. If they sold their land to the government, they would receive a cash annuity. When Choctaw chiefs signed the Treaty of Dancing Rabbit Creek, Choctaw land was given to the US government in exchange for land west of the Mississippi River. This decision was met with opposition by many Choctaw people who had no desire to leave their ancestral homes. Once the treaty was signed, the idea that Native people did not own their land circulated. Because of this and pressure from European settlers who wanted land, the treaty was ignored.

In 1831, the federal government began to forcibly remove Choctaw people from their homes. Though the removal lasted more than seventy years, the largest group, of approximately twelve thousand people, made the journey west from 1831 to 1834. They faced unimaginable hardships on the Trail of Tears across Mississippi to what is now eastern Oklahoma. Choctaw chief George Harkins, who experienced the journey, called it the "Trail of Tears and Death." Upon arrival, they began a new life. Choctaw people are strong and determined. Not only did they survive, but they kept their cultural values and traditions. Although means were limited, Choctaw looked to one another for support. They reestablished their government, developed towns, and built schools and churches.

IRISH POTATO FAMINE

A potato blight struck Ireland in 1845. The plant fungus *Phytophthora infestans* infected most of the potato crops. Potatoes were the main food source for poor Irish people, and when the crops failed, there was not enough to eat or sell. They could not pay rent and were evicted by English landlords. Their homes were burned. They had no shelter, no clean water, and little or no food, so disease and starvation followed.

An Irish farmer described the events of August 1845: "You could begin to see the tops of the potato stalks lying over as if the life was gone out of them. And that was the beginning of the great trouble and famine that destroyed Ireland." (John Millington Synge, *In Wicklow and West Kerry,* 1912.)

About a dozen years after Choctaw people arrived in Indian Territory, they heard of the famine in Ireland from an article in a newspaper. Choctaw sent what they could afford. Their gift was recorded in the Central Relief Committee of the Society of Friends ledger on May 21, 1847. It shows $170 given by "the children of the forest, our red brethren of the Choctaw nation." ("Choctaw and Irish History," www.choctawnation.com.)

Time passed, and the Choctaw people forgot about this gift, but it was never forgotten by the Irish. Irish oral and written histories memorialized the gift from the Choctaw people.

In the early 1990s, Ireland and the Choctaw Nation of Oklahoma began to communicate about the similarities in their histories under colonialism. The Choctaw Nation became aware of their ancestors' role in helping the Irish people.

The Midleton East Cork Town Council in Ireland met in 2013 and decided to commission a sculpture. *Kindred Spirits* by Alex Pentek was dedicated on June 18, 2017, in Midleton's Bailick Park. Councilor Seamus McGrath, the mayor of the County of Cork, proclaimed, "We have a shared past as people who have experienced unwelcome intrusion, and a shared sense of injustice." Choctaw Chief Gary Batton said, "We can celebrate overcoming diversity and our history as kindred spirits." ("Sculpture in Ireland Honors Choctaw Nation," www.stiglernews. com, July 5, 2017.)

When COVID-19 devastated the Navajo and Hopi Nations, social media ensured that information traveled quickly. People in Ireland heard about the fundraising effort to help. People in Ireland and Irish descendants in the United States donated over three million dollars in honor of the Choctaw gift seven generations earlier.

CHOCTAW NATION and IRELAND TODAY

Ireland and the Choctaw Nation of Oklahoma continue to maintain a special relationship. Both Nations suffered through conditions and situations out of their control. They lost a lot but still preserved their unique cultures and traditions. And with strong determination, the Irish and Choctaw peoples rescued their ancient languages from extinction.

Through a continuing series of annual scholarships, Choctaw students go to Ireland to study. This generosity of spirit will take the friendship of these two Nations well into future generations as acts of kindness continue being passed forward. ("Born Through a Donation 175 Years Ago the Choctaw-Irish Bond Remains Strong Today," www. choctawnation.com, March 2, 2022.)

Choctaw Chief Gary Batton explained, "Our word for their selfless act is 'iyyikowa'—it means serving those in need. We have become kindred spirits with the Irish in the years since the Irish Potato Famine. We hope the Irish, Navajo, and Hopi peoples develop lasting friend-ships, as we have. Sharing our cultures makes the world grow smaller." ("Choctaw and Irish History," www.choctawnation.com.)

TIME LINE

1830
Treaty of Dancing Rabbit Creek signed.

1831–1834
Trail of Tears takes place.

1832
Skullyville (from the Choctaw word iskulli or iskuli, meaning "money") established as first capital of the Choctaw Nation.

March 23, 1847
Skullyville Choctaws collect $170 for Irish Potato Famine relief.

November 16, 1907
Oklahoma becomes the forty-sixth US state, and the name "Indian Territory" is no longer used.

1845–1850
Potato crops fail, and Ireland's worst famine takes place.

1990
Choctaw officials participate in an annual walk in County Mayo to commemorate the Doolough Tragedy, a starvation march in Ireland during the famine.

KEY

CHOCTAW EVENT

IRISH EVENT

CHOCTAW and IRISH EVENT

June 18, 2017
Kindred Spirits statue dedication event is attended by a delegation including Choctaw Chief Gary Batton and Assistant Chief Jack Austin Jr.

1992
Irish activists and Choctaw officials retrace the Trail of Tears in a gesture of reciprocal solidarity to support starving Somali people.

1995
Irish President Mary Robinson visits the Choctaw Nation of Oklahoma to renew the friendship and to thank the Choctaw people for their aid.

2013
Irish sculptor Alex Pentek commissioned to design and build a commemorative sculpture.

2018
Irish Prime Minister Leo Varadkar visits the Choctaw Nation of Oklahoma and announces a scholarship program for young Choctaws to study in Ireland.

2020
The global COVID-19 pandemic has devastating effects on the Navajo and Hopi Nations, and Irish citizens contribute significantly toward relief.

~ GLOSSARY ~

Irish words

dadai (dah-dee): father

pratie (PRAW-tee): potato

mámámó (mah-mah-moh): grandmother

Choctaw words

halito (hah-leh-TOH): hello

Halito, chim achukma? (hah-leh-TOH, chem ah-CHOHK-mah): Hello, how are you?

shilombish ittibachvffa (she-LOHM-bish ite-teh-bah-CHAHF-fah): kindred spirits

tushpa (TUHSH-pah): hurry

LEARN MORE

I consulted many sources for this story: books, newspaper articles, videos, and personal conversations. Below are sources that young readers might find interesting. Use the internet to look for more information about the *Kindred Spirits* memorial and the relationship between the Choctaw and Irish people.

Bartoletti, Susan Campbell. *Black Potatoes: The Story of the Great Irish Famine*, 1845–1850. New York: Houghton Mifflin Harcourt, 2001.

"*Kindred Spirits*—The Choctaw-Irish Bond Lives On," ChoctawNationOK YouTube https://www.youtube.com/watch?v=dhO2sIRaDPc More information about both the Choctaw and Irish peoples' history.

"Making of *Kindred Spirits*," ChoctawNationOK YouTube https://www.youtube.com/watch?v=QLnrtcqFeCY The artist who created *Kindred Spirits* discusses his process for creating the sculpture.

Yurth, Cindy. "Irish 'Pay Forward' 173-Year-Old Favor." *Navajo Times / Diné bi Naaltsoos*, May 7, 2020. https://navajotimes.com/ae/community/irish-pay-forward-173-year-old-favor/ A story written in the Navajo tribal newspaper about donations from Irish people.

To all children: be proud of your heritage—L. S. W.

To all the Choctaw people with their big and kind hearts—J. Y.

Yakoke to Traci Sorell for the challenge to write this story; to my agent, Kelly Dysterhouse, for her encouragement; and to Terry, through thick and thin.—L. S. W.

Text copyright © 2024 by Leslie Stall Widener
Illustrations copyright © 2024 by Johnson Yazzie
All rights reserved, including the right of reproduction in whole or in part in any form.
Charlesbridge and colophon are registered trademarks of Charlesbridge Publishing, Inc.
At the time of publication, all URLs printed in this book were accurate and active. Charlesbridge, the author, and the illustrator are not responsible for the content or accessibility of any website.

Published by Charlesbridge • 9 Galen Street • Watertown, MA 02472 • (617) 926-0329 • www.charlesbridge.com

Library of Congress Cataloging-in-Publication Data
Names: Widener, Leslie Stall, author. | Yazzie, Johnson, illustrator.
Title: Kindred spirits: shilombish ittibachvffa / Leslie Stall Widener; illustrated by Johnson Yazzie.
Description: [Watertown, MA]: Charlesbridge, [2024] | Includes bibliographical references. | Audience: Ages 5–8 | Audience: Grades 2–3 | Summary: "Ireland, Choctaw Nation, Navajo Nation, and Hopi Nation: linked forever through generosity and care over almost two centuries from the Potato Famine to the Covid pandemic."—Provided by publisher.
Identifiers: LCCN 2023016270 (print) | LCCN 2023016271 (ebook) | ISBN 9781623543969 (hardcover) | ISBN 9781632893680 (ebook)
Subjects: LCSH: Choctaw Indians—History—Juvenile literature. | Ireland—History—Famine, 1845–1852—Juvenile literature. | Choctaw Nation of Oklahoma—Foreign economic relations—Ireland—Juvenile literature. | Ireland—Foreign economic relations—Choctaw Nation of Oklahoma—Juvenile literature. | Food relief—Ireland—History—19th century—Juvenile literature. | COVID-19 Pandemic, 2020—Social aspects—Southwestern States—Juvenile literature. | Navajo Indians—History—21st century—Juvenile literature. | Hopi Indians—History—21st century—Juvenile literature. | Solidarity—History—Juvenile literature. | Charity—Juvenile literature.
Classification: LCC E99.C8 W65 2024 (print) | LCC E99.C8 (ebook) | DDC 337.41507—dc23/eng/20230823
LC record available at https://lccn.loc.gov/2023016270
LC ebook record available at https://lccn.loc.gov/2023016271

Printed in China
(hc) 10 9 8 7 6 5 4 3 2 1

Illustrations done in in acrylic paints on canvas
Display type set in ITC Kallos by Phill Grimshaw
Text type set in Caspian by Marshall Bohlin
Color separations by Tom Alexander
Printed by 1010 Printing International Limited in Huizhou, Guangdong, China
Production supervision by Nicole Turner
Designed by Kristen Nobles